CITIZEN SCIENCE PROJECTS

Plant Projects

BY KARI A. CORNELL

Kids Core

An Imprint of Abdo Publishing
abdobooks.com

abdobooks.com

Printed in the United States of America, North Mankato, Minnesota.
102025
012026

THIS BOOK CONTAINS RECYCLED MATERIALS

Cover Photo: Shutterstock Images
Interior Photos: Andrii Nikitin/Shutterstock Images, 4–5; Anne Kitzman/Shutterstock Images, 7; Jared Quentin/Shutterstock Images, 9; Shutterstock Images, 10, 17, 18, 22 (insects), 22 (bird), 22 (bat), 25, 28 (top), 28 (bottom), 29 (top); Lucian Coman/Shutterstock Images, 12–13; Hatchapong Palurtchaivong/Shutterstock Images, 14; Makro Betz/Shutterstock Images, 20–21; Angelsu Kratob/Shutterstock Images, 23; Victoria Moloman/Shutterstock Images, 26; Pavel Kobysh/Shutterstock Images, 29 (bottom)

Editor: Trudy Becker
Series Designer: Marley Richmond

Library of Congress Control Number: 2025939876

Publisher's Cataloging-in-Publication Data

Names: Cornell, Kari A., author.
Title: Plant projects / by Kari A. Cornell
Description: Minneapolis, Minnesota: Abdo Publishing, 2026 | Series: Citizen science projects | Includes online resources and index.
Identifiers: ISBN 9781098298586 (lib. bdg.) | ISBN 9798384932383 (ebook)
Subjects: LCSH: Science projects--Juvenile literature. | Field experiments--Juvenile literature. | Plants--Juvenile literature. | Botany--Experiments--Juvenile literature. | Botany--Juvenile literature. | Ecology--Experiments--Juvenile literature. | Ecological science--Juvenile literature.
Classification: DDC 507.8--dc23

CONTENTS

Sagebrush does not need a lot of water. That means it can grow in dry landscapes.

CHAPTER 1

Saving Sagebrush

A group of fifth graders fanned out across the dry, rolling hills. The Pacific Ocean glimmered in the distance. The class was visiting Crystal Cove State Park near Laguna Beach, California. Under the hot sun, Natalia and Dylan scanned the ground.

They were searching for California sagebrush. This plant is native to the California coast. It has needlelike, silvery-green leaves and woody stems.

California sagebrush used to grow all over this **habitat**. But over time, the plant began to disappear. Years of farming, building, and more made the plant less common.

The fifth graders' class wanted to bring sagebrush back. A student from the University of California, Irvine, was helping. She taught the class how to spot plants that were not native to the area. Then the kids removed those plants. This would give sagebrush more room to grow. Rabbits also eat sagebrush leaves.

California sagebrush looks different throughout the year. In summer, the leaves may wilt or fall off.

The students put up fencing around the sagebrush to protect it.

Later in the season, the students came back. They measured how much the plants grew. They also measured the water level

Saving Habitats

Native plants are key parts of healthy habitats. They provide food and shelter to insects, birds, and other animals. Native plants can also prevent **erosion**. That is why it is important to save them. Citizen scientists can help find or track non-native plants. They can remove those plants. And volunteers can grow native plants.

California sagebrush can produce tiny flowers during spring and summer.

in the soil. There was good news. The plants were healthier than before! Their work had been good for the sagebrush. And their information helped scientists learn more about the habitat.

Citizen scientists do not need scientific training to help with projects.

Citizen Science

Natalia and Dylan's class was taking part in Project CRYSTAL. This is a citizen science project. In citizen science projects, regular people help gather information for scientific researchers.

In many projects, people **monitor** nature and report what they see. Then scientists use the information in their studies. They can research plants, animals, weather, and more. By gathering **data**, citizen scientists play a key role in scientific research.

Further Evidence

Look at the webpage below. Does it give any new evidence to support Chapter One?

California Sagebrush

abdocorelibrary.com/plant-projects

Some plants bloom in early spring. Others may not bloom until fall.

CHAPTER 2

Plants and Climate

Many citizen science projects focus on plants. In some, people report the first leaves or flower blooms that appear on plants in the spring. This data helps scientists learn more about the plants' life cycles. It also helps scientists track larger patterns.

Nature's Notebook volunteers should check their trees two to four times each week.

For example, scientists can learn more about how **climate change** is affecting different types of plants.

Green Wave

Each spring, many trees burst out in green leaves. This change is sometimes called the "green wave." In Nature's Notebook, citizen scientists help monitor the green wave.

Nature's Notebook volunteers choose one or more trees in their area to watch. In spring, they look for growing buds, unfolding leaves, and growing leaves. They check in fall too.

What Is Phenology?

Phenology is the study of natural events that happen regularly with the changing seasons, such as growing leaves or fruit. Scientists track when these events happen each year. In some years, plants grow leaves earlier or later than normal. That affects animals that need the plants for food.

Volunteers note colored or falling leaves. Then they record their findings. They use the Nature's Notebook mobile app or website.

Cherry Blossom Blitz

Cherry blossom trees are some of the earliest trees to bloom each spring. The trees are native to Japan. For around 1,200 years, people have kept records of their bloom. Scientists use this data to study climate change over time.

Budburst's Cherry Blossom Blitz is a citizen science program. People can gather data about cherry trees near their homes. Volunteers monitor the trees. Then they record the dates when the cherry blossoms appear.

In 2024, cherry blossom trees bloomed an average of two weeks earlier than they did in 1850.

There are many different types of cherry blossom trees. Cherry Blossom Blitz volunteers should find out what kind they are recording.

After that, scientists can compare these records. They can track changes from year to year. Or they can spot patterns across different areas of land.

Primary Source

Theresa Crimmins is a scientist. She created Nature's Notebook. She said:

> Answer as many or as few [questions] as you wish, and . . . every single record that we get is a really valuable piece of a huge quilt of data that we're stitching together.

Source: Margaret Roach. "Phenology with Theresa Crimmins." *A Way to Garden*, 21 Mar. 2025, awaytogarden.com. Accessed 28 July 2025.

Comparing Texts

Think about the quote. Does it support the information in this chapter? Or does it give a different perspective? Explain how in a few sentences.

A bee may visit thousands of flowers in one day.

CHAPTER 3

Plants Need Pollinators

Some plant projects focus on **pollinators**. Bees, flies, and butterflies are common pollinators. So are birds and beetles. Budburst's Summer Time Pollination is a citizen science project focused on that subject.

Common Pollinators

Many different animals can pollinate plants.

In the project, helpers track pollinators on flowers in their area. The data helps scientists compare pollinator numbers from year to year.

The Summer Time Pollination project happens from June through August each year. Citizen scientists watch nearby plants for ten minutes each day. If they spot a pollinator, they note the name, place, and date. Volunteers also record information about the plants the pollinator visited. They record the plant's name and size.

Budburst volunteers can record information about the weather, such as temperature and cloud cover.

They also count the number of open flowers and see how far each one has opened.

Nectar Connectors

Most flowering plants need pollinators in order to grow fruit. But pollinators also rely on those plants. For example, monarch butterflies need milkweed plants for **nectar**. Nectar Connectors is a project through Nature's Notebook.

Bees and Blooms

Some insects such as bees are not active in colder months. If plants bloom too early, the insects may still be resting. This means the plants may not get pollinated. Then those plants cannot make fruit or seeds. When the insects become active, they may have trouble finding food.

Plants such as apple trees must bloom in spring in order to make fruit in fall.

It collects data about when 53 types of nectar plants bloom.

Helpers do an online training first. Then they find nectar plants nearby. They choose the type of plants they want to watch. Next, they visit those plants while they are flowering. Volunteers record when the buds swell up. They note when the first flower appears. They also note the last flower, first ripe fruit, and lost leaves. Volunteers enter all this data online.

Buds on the same plant may not open at the same time.

Scientists carefully consider this data. They see if bloom time matches when pollinators are gathering nectar. If researchers spot a problem, they can try to find solutions.

Nectar Connectors is just one way for regular people to assist scientific research. Many projects give plant lovers a chance to help. They can work to protect plants for the future.

Explore Online

Read about honeybees at the website below. Is there any information that wasn't in Chapter Three?

Honeybees

abdocorelibrary.com/plant-projects

Science Projects

Citizen scientists participating in Cherry Blossom Blitz must have cherry blossoms nearby to monitor.

Citizen scientists tracking pollinators for Budburst need internet access to submit their data.

Citizen scientists watching plants for Nectar Connectors need to take a training course online.

Citizen scientists tracking specific types of plants must be able to identify the plant in nature.

Glossary

climate change
a dangerous long-term change in Earth's temperature and weather patterns

data
information

erosion
the process of land being moved or broken down by water, wind, and ice

habitat
the natural environment where a plant or animal lives

monitor
to watch or keep track of

nectar
a sweet liquid produced by plants

pollinator
an animal that helps plants produce seeds by moving pollen from one flower to another

Online Resources

To learn more about plant projects, visit our free resource websites below.

Core Library CONNECTION
FREE! COMMON CORE MULTIMEDIA RESOURCES

Visit **abdocorelibrary.com** or scan this QR code for free Common Core resources for teachers and students, including vetted activities, multimedia, and booklinks, for deeper subject comprehension.

Booklinks NONFICTION NETWORK
FREE! ONLINE NONFICTION RESOURCES

Visit **abdobooklinks.com** or scan this QR code for free additional online weblinks for further learning. These links are routinely monitored and updated to provide the most current information available.

Learn More

Bell, Samantha S. *Pollinator Gardens*. Abdo, 2026.

Debbink, Andrea. *Flowers and Plants*. Abdo, 2022.

Hoare, Ben. *The Secret World of Plants*. DK, 2022.

Index

About the Author

Kari A. Cornell is an award-winning children's book author who gardens, runs, and makes pottery. She lives in Minneapolis with her husband and their sweet dog, EmmyLou.